Business and Salesmanship

By

JOEL S. GOLDSMITH

Martino Publishing
Mansfield Centre, CT
2011

Martino Publishing
P.O. Box 373,
Mansfield Centre, CT 06250 USA

www.martinopublishing.com

ISBN   978-1-61427-196-3

© 2011 Martino Publishing

Cover design by T. Matarazzo

Printed in the United States of America On 100% Acid-Free Paper

Business and Salesmanship

By

JOEL S. GOLDSMITH

WILLING PUBLISHING CO.
San Gabriel, California

*"Unless the Lord build the house, they
labor in vain that build it."*

Psalm 127

Illumination dissolves all material ties and binds
men together with the golden chains of spiritual
understanding; it acknowledges only the leadership
of the Christ; it has no ritual or rule but the divine,
impersonal universal Love; no other worship than the
inner Flame that is ever lit at the shrine of Spirit.
This union is the free state of spiritual brotherhood.
The only restraint is the discipline of Soul, therefore we know liberty without license; we are a united
universe without physical limits; a divine service to
God without ceremony or creed. The illumined walk
without fear—by Grace.

(From the book, *"The Infinite Way.")*

BUSINESS

Business always seems to be dependent on certain conditions, circumstances and seasons, or on the good will of other persons. In the human picture business is effected by weather, finances, changing modes and fads, but turning from this picture we find that in reality business is the continuous activity of Principle; that this activity is infinite and harmonious, and that it is maintained and sustained by Principle itself.

Christian metaphysics, revealing the spiritual nature of business, aids us to lift our thoughts regarding all commercial activity to the place where the true idea of business is apprehended. Every idea, and your business is an idea of Mind, is supported by the animating Principle of the idea. "When an idea begins to work in thought, it furnishes all that is necessary for its equipment, establishment and nourishment."

ADAM DICKEY.

5

BUSINESS AND SALESMANSHIP

Business is an infinite activity, is forever without limit, and is never dependent on person, place or thing. Right where you are, business is. It is a result of and resident in individual consciousness, because individual consciousness is the universal Consciousness individually expressed. If we go about our tasks doing those things that lie nearest at hand, with faith that there is an ever-present, invisible power which the Hebrews call Emmanuel, or "God with us," and which Christians call the Christ, our work will always bear fruit.

This omnipresent and omnipotent power is the Presence of God prospering all right endeavor. It is only in the degree which we believe that it is either some personal effort of our own or another's, or that it is the good will of humans that prospers us, which causes apparent failure or lessening of fruitful activity. The prophet Isaiah clearly reminds us to "cease ye from man whose breath is in his nostrils, for wherein is he to be accounted for."

The point to remember is that at all times, and in all places, there is an invisible and omnipotent power acting to support every right human effort; and the way to demonstrate this is recognize and acknowledge the presence and power of God and rely on it.

Business, spiritually understood, is the reverse of the usual conception in which every thought must be held to profit and loss and good policy and bad policy, or that which is or that which is not "good business." This business is never at the mercy of times and tides or circumstances and conditions, but is the free flow of the activity of Mind universally expressed.

Lack and limitation exist only in the belief that God and man have become separated from each other. The true understanding of man's relationship to God reveals the ever-presence of supply, the immediate availability of good in every form and in an unlimited quantity.

Spiritual truths cannot be intellectually discerned, yet they may be unfolded to our consciousness as the result of understanding thoughts received from the intellect. Before we can understand the meaning of at-one-ment with God, we must learn of our real relationship to Life, and for this purpose we may use a material symbol, as, let us say, a diamond.

Every cut diamond has numerous facets. Not only is it true that each facet is part of the diamond, but actually there can never be any separation between the facet and the diamond, because the diamond and the facet is one, one piece, one object, one whole.

If you can visualize the relationship between the facets and the diamond, you will, even though faintly, catch a glimpse of your inseparability from God. You will note that every facet expresses the life, fire, color and quality of the whole diamond; that each facet reflects the purity and the quality of the gem; and that the entire activity and all the beauty and durability of the stone is expressed in each individual facet, and never is any single facet detached or detachable from the whole gem. Beauty, color, fire, character, quality and strength are inherent in the diamond and it expresses each and all of these attributes through every facet. The facet, then, is the outlet for the shining forth of the gem's brilliancy.

In like manner the supply of life, health, substance, strength and purity, which are the constituted qualities of divine Mind, are forever being expressed by Mind through each and every idea, man and the whole universe.

The facet of the diamond need not pray for color or brilliance because the diamond has no power to withhold these from its outer surface. This illustration makes plain why Spirit cannot withhold its supply of life, its quality of substance, activity and peace, from its individualized being.

Everything needful for the brightness and permanency of the facet is within the stone and is forever expressing itself. All that man can ever need is within the universal Mind, eternal Life, and is pouring itself into expression through man every moment.

In the case of the diamond it is only necessary to keep the surface of the stone, the facets, clean — and the fire within shines forth in its perfection. In the case of man he needs only to keep his thought clear of the mists of fear and doubt — and the infinite supply inherent in his being will pour forth in abundant measure.

Too much effort is made by metaphysicians to *establish* at-one-ment with God, when the fact is that man can no more be separated from God, Love, Life, Mind or supply than the facet of the gem can be separated from the whole stone, or any of its qualities. Man is forever at-one with his good, God,— he needs but to know it. Nor can the life, substance or harmonious activity of Mind be withheld from any of its individualized expressions, if we rest in the consciousness of our true relationship with the source of our good.

SALESMANSHIP

SCIENTIFIC CHRISTIANITY has revealed to human thought the present possibility of health and success. It has shown us how to think and live so as to individualize the power of Spirit, God, and how to utilize the laws of Mind with which to establish and maintain the harmony of mind, body and business.

One of the outstanding facts learned through the study and application of Truth to human affairs, concerns the subject of salesmanship. All our earthly experiences involves to some extent the ability to sell. Many are actively engaged in selling commodities or services, as a means of earning a living. The understanding of Truth is of vital importance to these "ambassadors of trade" as salespeople are often called.

We ordinarily think of selling as the disposition of goods or services to another for a sum of money or for some other form of trade. The best salesman is believed to be the one who can dispose of the most goods, or secure the highest prices for his product. These goals are attained in various ways, some of them ethical, others called "high pressure salesmanship" which would not be considered in a business conducted according to the Golden Rule.

The student of Truth would always be the most successful salesman if he rightly understood and applied the laws of Mind in his work. Christian scientific selling can never meet with failure. It knows no "bad seasons" or "rainy weather" or "unseasonable weather" or any other of the innumerable excuses or alibis that are frequently given instead of orders.

The beginning of our understanding, or the starting point, is this: There is but one Mind and this Mind is the Mind of individual man. Therefore the Mind of the buyer is the Mind of the seller; the Mind of the customer is the Mind of the storekeeper; the Mind of the designer, the manufacturer, the wholesaler, retailer and ultimate consumer is the one and the same Mind, the ONLY Mind, individually expressed.

12

The importance of this fundamental understanding becomes clear when we learn that in this one Mind was conceived the idea which we desire to sell, and where also the idea was brought to fruition. This Mind operating in the customer recognized the good in your product, thereby completing the transaction, or rather, it reveals the transaction as already complete in Mind AND IN MANIFESTATION.

The belief that there are separate minds is the devil in salesmanship as it is also in every other phase of human experience. This belief in many minds leads us to the presumption that salespeople must convince the prospective buyer of the merits of their product. They sometimes misrepresent or exaggerate in order to sound convincing, and all this because of the mistaken belief that the Mind of the prospect is other than the Mind of the seller. When it is understood that the ONE Mind is operating as all parties it becomes plain to us that in this Mind there are no conflicting interests, no opposing thoughts, no interfering persons or circumstances. In this oneness of Mind no one idea can interfere with another; no one idea can hinder the right development and progress of another.

This prepares us for the unfoldment of the next step: What are ideas? Metaphysics explains all that exists, does so as ideas. It claims that sun, moon, stars, planets, plants, animals and man exist as ideas—ideas of the one Mind, God. It shows that these ideas are emanations of Mind, and "live and move and have their being" in God, Mind. In this Mind or infinite Consciousness, exists individual man, and all that pertains to him. In this Consciousness is embraced the idea of business, of invention, of art and the sciences. This Consciousness includes also the various manifestations of weather, seasons and climates. Modes and methods of trans-process of thought are revealed to human process of thought are revealed to human apprehension.

Mind, the source of all intelligence, is necessarily intelligent in its action, and therefore all the ideas of Mind are held in harmonious relationship to other ideas. From this it can readily be seen that one idea of Mind, let us say weather, could not act as a hindrance to another idea, business. Also, as each idea is dependent on its source, Mind, for existence and continuity, it is clear that the idea, business, can in no wise be dependent on any other idea for its good. Individuals, likewise, are dependent on God, divine Love, only, and can never be dependent on payroll, on the good will of persons, or the whims of circumstance. No sale of a legitimate product can be at the mercy of prejudice, bribery, ignorance or personality.

Salesmen sometimes have problems regarding rightful remuneration for their services. Here also it is necessary to remember that there is one Mind, and in this Mind there is no false activity, no selfish or dishonest thought or deed; that this Mind does recognize the true value of every idea. From this Consciousness only comes the proper reward or compensation for all right endeavor, and we need never look to person for this recognition or reward.

In presenting a proposition of any rightful nature we should hold to the truth that we are not presenting it to "man whose breath is in his nostrils," but to Mind. This Mind individualized as man is your prospect, your customer, your employer or employee. Trusting in the infinite nature and character of Mind, God, we find revealed all good in Mind's ideas. Relying on the integrity of the divine Being, we encounter this quality in individual man, the perfect image and likeness of eternal Being. This Principle reveals to us that whatever we recognize and acknowledge as the qualities and character of divine Love, we find manifested in Love's reflection, individual man and the universe. The Truth we realize as pertaining to Mind we experience in manifestation, because "I and my Father are one."